A Buzzard
in the Proper State
of Deadness

Also by Jeff Coomer

A Potentially Quite Remarkable Thursday

A Buzzard
in the Proper State
of Deadness

poems by
Jeff Coomer

Last Leaf PRESS
• Chestertown, MD •

Last Leaf
PRESS

Chestertown, MD
Printed in the United States of America.

FIRST PAPERBACK EDITION

Series Editor: Jeff Coomer
Layout and Design Editor: Sarah Crossland

Library of Congress Control Number: 2018956858
Last Leaf Press, Chestertown, MD

ISBN 978-0-9965708-2-4

To Emily and Tris,
long may you run

Table of Contents

Three

"Thank you, dear God, for this good life and forgive us if we do not love it enough."

—Garrison Keillor

One

The Witness

A friend is telling me about the fire
that severely damaged a bank on the main road
out of the town we live in. *You know,*
he says as I smile hopefully back at him,
the bank that's next to the new dentist's office
and right across from the Tastee Freeze.
I nod and say *hmmm*, but the truth is
that I don't *hmmm*; I don't *hmmm* at all,
even though I must have driven by the place
he's mentioned hundreds of times.
In the coming days I notice how atrocious
I also am at remembering names and faces
and the year something happened,
much less the details of the something
it is that's alleged to have happened
in the year that escapes me.
It's troubling to realize what an unreliable
witness I make to the life I'm living—
whatever small satisfaction I might take
in not being able to convict myself of any crimes
offset by the unease I feel at never
having a good alibi for my whereabouts.

Spoiler Alert

You will not be elected President
or fulfill any of the other prophecies
scrawled in the pages of the yearbook
you're holding. None of the people
who wished they'd gotten to know you better
is ever going to know you any better
than they do right now. Faster than
you'd believe possible, your legendary group
of amigos will scatter like the shards
of a dropped bottle of Boone's Farm
strawberry wine; even your best friend
eventually spins into a corner out of sight.
The girl who pledged she would "heart" you 4ever
is the first to go.

But on the first day of the second semester
of your dismal freshman year at college,
raise your gaze to take note of the girl
with glasses and long brown hair
who's waiting in the dinner line ahead of you.
She's talking with two of her friends.
Write it all down. Forty years later
you'll look up at the stars in a coal-black
autumn sky and try to remember every detail
of that moment. You'll kick yourself
for not taking more photographs,
and another poetry class or two.

Boys with Matches

A Story with Miracles

This is what passed for a terrific idea
to three eleven-year-old boys bored
with exploring the vacant fields behind
their houses on a March afternoon:
we would light a fire and put it out
by peeing on it. All three of us
had matches (why would we not?),
and we were standing knee-high
in an abundance of combustible material;
what we didn't have, as it turned out,
was enough command over our bladders
to pee while stepping backward.
Rapidly.

The first miracle of that day was that we
stomped out the flames with the help
of some good-natured construction workers
after only an acre or so had burned.
The second miracle was that nobody
called the police or fire department
at any point in the proceedings.
The third miracle was that all six
of our parents agreed we were heroes
for helping the construction workers

put out the fire that had spread from
the trash they were carelessly burning.

In gratitude for our good fortune,
that afternoon was the last time any of us
played with fire; at least the kind
you start with matches.

Lost

How impossibly quaint it now seems,
my best friend and I speeding down
moonlit backroads in his father's car,
no satellite pinging our location
onto a little screen, no soothing voice
instructing us to make a left
or right turn in two-tenths of a mile.
Half the roads we roamed
on those nights were too small
for the official state highway map
we might or might not have found
in the glove compartment.
It didn't matter. We made our way
by dead reckoning, gut instinct,
and dumb luck, and usually ended up
right about where we thought we would.
Though that didn't matter
a whole lot, either.

Big Plans

Smile all you like, but I am SERIOUS this time.
I'm done with shaving every day and I'm growing
my hair long, like it was in our college days.
I've been thinking about putting a tent
in the Subaru and taking a trip by myself
for two or even three weeks (probably New Mexico
but possibly Canada), or I might just pedal
all the way to Colorado on backroads
like I said I was going to do ten years ago
(it would take me approximately 38 days,
which includes some days off for rain and to rest).
You can follow along in the car if you want to
(that would be entirely up to you), but if you
decide to stay home, I've read somewhere
that loads of people living on the main route
will give passing cyclists a square meal
and a place to sleep. Completely FREE,
out of the goodness of their hearts. Or I'll sleep
in a field in one of those lightweight tents
I've seen advertised online (obviously I will also
have to buy paniers for my bike to carry such items),
and then in the evenings I'll strip down
and bathe myself in a nearby pond or river.
I'm not afraid of being seen naked in such circumstances.
It's only a misdemeanor in most states,
and if you aren't around to come fetch me
I'll call your brother, or one of the kids.
(I'm so glad you are enjoying this.)

Road Rage

As mad as I am that an idiot
in a sports car has positioned himself
within an inch of my bumper,
I'm even more pissed off
that he knows me well enough
to take for granted that I am not
going to risk serious injury
to either of us by slamming on
the brakes while he's hovering there.
What pisses me off most of all,
though, is that I've let an idiot
in a sports car make me as mad
as I feel at that moment.

After he whips around me
and races down the interstate,
I find myself enjoying the prospect
of coming across him again
in another few miles,
upside down and in a ditch,
preferably engulfed in flames
that remove all doubt.

You might guess that I'd be
thoroughly ashamed of myself
for wishing such a terrible fate

on another human being,
even an idiot, but you would be
wrong; I'd refer to it more as
"moderate disappointment."

Snakes

You can't spend most of your day
in their natural habitat and expect
not to see them every now and then,
usually the drab, harmless types,
but occasionally a copperhead.
Sure, I knew they served a useful purpose
in holding down the population
of small rodents, but the best I was
ever able to manage in their presence
was a sort of sweaty nonchalance.
I abhorred their cold, unblinking eyes
and mouths fixed in a false smile;
the way they lay coiled for hours
before slithering off into the shadows;
their habit of suddenly appearing
right in the middle of my path—
or, worst of all, seated in the front row
of a wood-paneled conference room
as I was about to begin a presentation
of the utmost importance.

What to Do, What to Do

Some days you just feel like giving up on the world—
not because of all the crap you read in the news
over breakfast, but because of the food wrappers
blowing across the sidewalk on your walk into town,
and the piles of real crap calcifying in the grass
at the park. This morning I'm ready to move
to a cabin in the woods where I can live off the grid
and grow my own vegetables, which the rabbits and deer
will leave alone because they have so much else to eat.
There won't be any snakes around, either.
For the rest of my walk I entertain myself by mapping out
my future home and plot of land in great detail,
though I know full well I'm going to keep on doing
what I've always done; walk past the crap
and pick up the wrappers.

Mornings at Me, Incorporated

The Accountant is always the first to arrive,
30 minutes before the alarm sounds,
late night out or not, weekends included.
He's at his desk even earlier this morning,
tsk-tsking his way through yesterday's
credits and debits, searching in vain
for any shred of documentation
that might explain the alarming spike
in miscellaneous expenses. Lately,
he's been demanding that I allocate time
for a line-by-line review of something
he refers to as my "balance sheet."
*You need to start making an effort
to understand this stuff,* he tells me
with a genuine sense of urgency,
but I cover my face and say no,
that's why *he's* there; everyone knows
I'm more of a big-picture,
delegate-downward kind of guy.
And that's not a liability, I add,
pushing past him for the snooze button,
it's a goddamn asset.

Sandwiches Made "Fresh" Daily

After three weeks of rolling my eyes
at the handwritten sign taped to the door,
I go in for a sandwich and a friendly chat
with the owner, who clearly needs
to be advised that his inappropriate use
of quotation marks is in fact calling
the freshness of his wares into question.
Someone, I think, must carry the flag
for precision in grammar and punctuation,
and who better than I (a published poet
and acknowledged master of the semi-colon)
to fulfill such a duty on this fine May afternoon?
Perhaps the owner will even refuse to accept
my payment when he grasps the impact
his error has been having on his business;
a gesture I would naturally decline.
Oh, please, I will say with a modest wave
of my hand, *it's all in a day's work*
for a published poet.

While I eat my sandwich (chicken salad
on whole wheat) I consider whether
I should recommend that the owner underline
the word "fresh" to achieve the emphasis
he desires, or italicize it. (He could, of course,
also use all capital letters.) In the end, however,

I decide it would be best to defer the matter
to a day that's less busy; a day when I also
don't have a large spot of mayonnaise
on the crotch of my pants.

Gunslingers

You see it all the time in the old Westerns on TV—
a good cowboy is brooding over a whiskey in a saloon
when three bad cowboys at a nearby table
start abusing a tainted but kind-hearted woman
named Kate who works there. The good cowboy
crashes his glass down on the bar and saunters over.
The crowd scatters. Hands hover over pistols.
There's an exchange of sideways squints and threats
which ends when the bad cowboys slink off to plot
their revenge. The piano music resumes, slowly.

Every time I watch this scene I end up annoyed
by the good cowboy's eagerness to kill or be killed
defending Kate's honor. I want to know whether
his father was equally impetuous, and whether
he and Kate have a secret history that ended badly
before the opening credits. Does Kate remind
the good cowboy of his first love (or his mother)?
He may not have a wife and kids, but is there *nothing*
in his life important enough to tip the scale against
risking everything for Kate's (already damaged) honor?
Would the good cowboy be as quick to confront
the bad cowboys if he knew Kate had recently been
diagnosed with terminal cancer? What if *he*
had recently been diagnosed with terminal cancer?

I'd like to think that being nearsighted is the reason
I wouldn't make a good gunslinger, but really—
it's needing to ask questions like these.

What's the Matter

I'm resting in an October landscape
contemplating how it is possible
that an uncountable collection of atoms
could organize themselves into this moment—
yellow leaves meandering through
damp air to the ground below,
the faint song of a stream trickling
over a bed of gray stones, me perched
on a boulder with a consciousness
able to appreciate it all.

I can't say I really know what an atom
even is anymore; my last point of reference
is a drawing of fuzzy electron planets
orbiting a lumpy sun of protons and neutrons.
But now there are leptons and bosons,
gluons, gravitons, and six (I swear this is
the actual scientific term) *flavors* of quarks,
some collection of which may be
creating reality by vibrating like the strings
in a cosmic orchestra. Or possibly
that's something else altogether.

This morning my consideration
of such weighty matters fails to bring me
into closer communion with anything
I've come across hanging above an altar.

It leaves me just as far, though, from everyone
who's absolutely certain that my sitting here
thinking about anything at all is entirely
a matter of chemistry and physics.

Commencement

None of the speakers who stepped up
to the podium that night had the wisdom
or heart to tell us how much we were
already what we would become.
No one who drank Coke would switch to Pepsi,
no one who didn't already smoke would decide to start.
The class smart-asses would snicker their way
through multiple jobs and marriages
while the congenial plodders turtle-crawled
to houses like the ones they grew up in.
Most of the kids with the money to leave town
for college would leave town for good.
Everyone with a serious issue to work through
would still be working on it when their hair turned gray.
The statistically correct number of us
would die before fifty and make it to ninety.
Whatever our expiration date, the songs we knew
by heart on that magnificent spring evening
would be the ones we'd hum alone in our kitchens
right up to the end.

Conifers of the Northeastern U.S.

Who knows why she fell in love
with conifers as a young newlywed
those many years ago, but she did;
and after a lifetime of reading,
snapping pictures, and cataloguing
the copious cone and needle specimens
she collected on weekend excursions
to every corner of the surrounding states,
she was the undisputed local expert
on all things coniferous, a frequent
and (those who knew her best would say)
surprisingly engaging guest speaker
on the regional gardening club circuit.

Some Sunday mornings in church
she fretted about whether all the time
and money she'd devoted to conifers
would not have been better spent on things
of more direct benefit to those in need.
Yet—wasn't it Jesus himself who proclaimed
that the poor would always be with us?
And who among even the grievously poor
would not say their burdens were lightened
by the scent of pine on an April morning,
the spires of spruce and fir that pierce
the gray days of winter?

A Mouse Tale

Though only of average size,
he somehow managed to maneuver
an entire foil-wrapped Hershey's kiss
off the edge of a high pantry shelf,
heave and haul it over great open plains
of parquet and carpet, and finally,
through sheer force of gritty will,
push it down cliff face after cliff face
to the bottom of the basement steps—

an achievement I readily acknowledge
as being more worthy of praise
than my use of the kiss to bait the trap
I'm now carrying past the trash can
to a little hole I've dug next to a rose bush
in the backyard; the only act of grace
hindsight allows.

A Church Lesson

Joe and Marge—
we met them at a progressive dinner
organized by the women's group
of the church we'd joined as newlyweds.
They were much older, early fifties,
and both on their second marriage;
by every appearance happy in the new life
they were making together, and easy
for us to talk to. From that night on,
we waved to them across the pews
and exchanged friendly small talk
anytime we saw them at church events.

A year or so after that first meeting
we noticed that Joe was often in church alone,
though still smiling as he always did
and with his usual leisurely wave.
Before we got around to asking,
we overheard someone whisper cancer.
When the dreaded Sunday came
that neither Joe nor Marge was in church,
the congregation was stunned
to learn it was Joe who had died,
from a massive heart attack the night before.
Marge followed a month later.

You can, of course, make of their story
as much or as little as you choose; for my part,
they're the only two people I remember
from our years in that church,
except for the priest.

Leaving

Feeling a need for ritual
I walked our land one last time
the evening before we left,
pausing as I went to take back
the names we'd bestowed when
the place first became ours—
Witches Pond and *Fern Path*;
Front Meadow, *Rock Face*,
and *Lightning Tree*; the *Dying Ash*.
In the soft ground by the creek
I dug a hole to make a ceremonial burial
of the work gloves I'd held together
with duct tape, the lumberjack hat
with ear flaps everyone laughed at me
for wearing well into spring,
and three autumn olive branches
squeezed by honeysuckle into shapes
resembling wizard's wands.

Susan, who is far more expert
in such matters than I, would no doubt
have chosen the finality of flames,
the lightness of smoke carrying
the past up into the heavens;
but in that moment it was
all I could do to scrape the dirt
back over my offering,
and breathe.

Bargains

Over the years I've proposed more than
my share of them to whatever higher power
I was communing with at the time,
each offer born of a desperation so deep
even the memory of them tightens my chest.
Please please/If only you will/I will—
the three-part template of the contract
I put forward from the moment I rose
in the morning until I was back in bed
trying to lie still enough for sleep.
What shames me now is that
I can remember all the things
I asked for and did or did not receive,
but nothing of what I promised;
except the pledge I pinned to the end
of every offer, that I would never,
never ask for anything again.

Two Trees

I'm sitting in my woods contemplating
two trees a short distance in front of me.
The first, a yellow poplar, is the picture
of good fortune, rising out of the rich bottomland
of the creek, holding court over the hickories
and oaks it outraced to the sun; a trunk
straight as an obelisk and not a single branch
within shouting distance of the ground.
The second tree, a black cherry, twists out
of the schist on the steep slope above the creek.
Its burled trunk arcs ungracefully back
toward the water, a single large limb stretching
in the same direction as if to break a fall.
The gnarled branches on the high side flail
this way and that in a valiant attempt to shake off
a tangle of grapevines and bittersweet.
Though the cherry is blocking the trail I'm making,
it's the poplar I have the urge to take down.

What Muskrat Tastes Like

During a lull in the conversation at my table,
I overhear one of the two well-dressed women

of a certain age sitting behind me say that
she recently spotted a rather large muskrat

swimming in the marsh near her summer house.
Her companion dabs her lips with her napkin

and observes that she's eaten muskrat
on several occasions, both fried and in stews.

And what would you say it tastes like?,
the first woman inquires while swirling her wine.

Squirrel, the second woman responds
after the briefest of pauses for reflection.

Her answer impresses me as the kind I hope
to give when I've attained a certain age,

and one I'm especially grateful for on this night,
having just ordered the chicken.

The Dead Buzzard

This evening I walk by an older couple enjoying
a cheese plate and some wine in their back garden.
Forty feet overhead, a dead buzzard dangles
from a branch in the tree that shades them.
It's hanging by a rope attached to its feet,
a position that causes its wings to splay so wide
you can't miss seeing it, which, the man in the garden
tells me, is precisely the point. He's quite proud
of the ingenuity it took to acquire a buzzard
in the proper state of deadness and then hoist it
so high up into the tree. Before he put it there,
he and his wife couldn't use the garden for all the shit
left by the fifty buzzards that had begun roosting
in the tree like clockwork every night at dusk.
You can look it up if you don't believe me, the man says—
a dead buzzard is the only thing proven to keep
other buzzards from taking up residence in a tree.
It makes sense, I answer, they're very smart birds.
I applaud his resourcefulness and continue on my walk,
pleased to be living in a world where hanging
an upside-down dead buzzard overhead
could improve someone's situation.

Two

Wondering About Things

Everyone used to have some talent for it,
like memorizing telephone numbers
and expressing thoughts in paragraphs.
My cousins and I once played an entire game
of Monopoly while our fathers chain-smoked Marlboros
and argued about the seventeen possible ways
of driving from some named point A to some other
named point B or C, not, of course, that any of them
had ever made such a trip or would likely need to.
My friends and I mastered speculation trying
to fill in the ocean of blanks remaining after
extended examination of three spaghetti-stained
Playboys we came across in a neighbor's trash can.
In college, I managed to keep myself awake
in a crappy summer desk job by wondering what
the girl I was dating had done on the previous day,
or earlier that morning, or at the precise instant
I had started wondering about her.

Perhaps it's my nostalgia for a world with room
for the pleasing ache of not instantly knowing
that's led me deep into the woods this morning,
to a spot by the creek where a big oak leans
precariously over the water. Every time it rains
the current exposes a little more of the roots
that have held the tree upright for longer than

I've been alive. It's my opinion that the next big storm
will be the one to finally bring it down.
Or maybe not; I've been saying the same thing
for quite some time now.

Astonishment

The young woman seated next to me at dinner
is astonished to learn that my wife and I
arranged our dates during summer breaks
from college by mailing *letters*,
which we hand-wrote on paper and still have
tucked away in a box somewhere.
Phone booths also amaze her, and the red dye
they used to put on pistachio shells.

I can't say her astonishment astonishes me—
after all, whole swaths of my father's youth
are as distant from my experience of the world
as my experience is from hers.
But the pleasure I feel in astonishing her
is tempered by a sadness almost like grief.
Perhaps she senses that in my rambling description
of how I would retreat to my room to read
and re-read those college letters while listening
to my favorite records, a bayberry candle
burning on my desk. Whatever the reason,
she soon turns her attention to the young man
sitting across from her, leaving me

to the entirely pleasurable experience
of imagining her face in the instant she recalls
our conversation forty years from now,

right after she's said something that astonishes
the yet-to-be-born young man
seated next to her.

Moment on a Brick Walk

How strange it is to stand again
on the same brick walk
I so often hurried down
half a lifetime ago, a stack of books
balanced under one arm,
my narrow shoulders bent
with the weight of a future
I didn't know whether I should
run to or from. In a spot
where only the size of the trees
has changed, I close my eyes,
breathe in the November air,
and try to feel again exactly
what I felt on those distant mornings
when every path seemed
long enough to need hurrying down.
It's impossible, of course;
not because of what the years
have faded from my memory,
but because of all they've added.
I stand on the walk a while longer,
eyes open, breathing in the air,
appreciating the only moment any of us
can ever be sure of knowing.

Presto!

I'm strolling down a busy city street
appreciating the beauty
of a sunny Monday morning,
unnoticed once again
by the equally beautiful people
swiping and pecking their way
past me to cubicles
and coffee shops and retail counters.
It's no different when
our paths cross in those places.
For a while I thought
I must have become invisible,
but every time I checked
I was as solid and shiny an object
as I've always been.
On further investigation,
I determined it was actually
everybody else who had become ghosts.
Fortunately, I found I can
make them materialize in front of me
by wearing unusual color combinations
and repeating an incantation
that begins with *Good Morning*
or *Good Evening*; a few stubborn cases
may also require three loud
finger snaps.

The Spider

A spider hangs motionless
from the corner of the plant stand
by the chair where I'm reading.
He—or is it *she*?—is small and brown
with long, translucent legs
tucked tightly beneath its body,
as though it's sensed my gaze
and is doing what it can to avoid detection.
Or perhaps it's picked up
the faint electrochemical signal
of what my seeing it has made me think about—
which is the number of spiders
I've killed over the years
for the minor sins of startling me
or daring to take up residence in my space,
or, worst of all, simply because *I could*.
Is it the laziness of advancing age
that keeps me from crushing
my present companion in a Kleenex?
Or the realization that it's no more
a danger to me than the gnats
it hopes to catch, and is destined
to die in a week or so anyway,
probably inside a vacuum cleaner bag?
No—what inspires me to now
carefully lift the spider back

onto the plant is the sudden flush
of kinship I feel from remembering
exactly what it's like to be in his—
or is it *her*?—position.

Cleopatra

I'm having a leisurely afternoon coffee
with the third woman I've known
who at some point in the conversation
leans close to reveal that she was Cleopatra—
yes, *the* Cleopatra—in a previous life.

I'm not an expert on the migration of souls,
but it occurs to me that at least two of the women
are almost certainly wrong; on the other hand,
I'd have to acknowledge that all three
do display the sort of regal disregard
and self-absorption one would expect to find
in the Queen of the Nile.

My current Cleopatra, for example,
doesn't show the least interest in who
I might have been in a former life.
Perhaps that's just as well, since all I could
tell her is that I have a recurring dream
of tending sheep in Scotland, and I'm convinced
that somewhere along the way one of me
drowned. I'm pleased, too, that I sense myself
trending in the right direction.

When People Say They Haven't Seen Me in a While

I nod and say yes, I know, I haven't
seen me in quite some time either,
and it's not that I haven't been looking
as I've accumulated a long list of issues
I urgently need to discuss with me,
and while addressing some of those issues
is bound to prove contentious,
I would like it duly noted that I have always
maintained a deep and abiding fondness
for me, I mean I genuinely *miss me*
when I'm not around me for any length of time,
and in spite of all that I've put up with
over the years on account of me,
I must still say that I can't think of anyone
who's been quite as good to me
as yours very truly.

Apology to My Nose

So much to ask forgiveness for—
the cheap jokes about your size
that bombed as self-effacing humor,
all the times I let slow traffic
or an idiot customer service rep
knock you out of joint.
Too often I've stuck you
into someone else's business
and held you to the grindstone
until you were raw; I've refused
to wake up after you smelled the coffee,
and joyfully eaten the meals
you warned me were fishy.
To my small credit, I always
carried a handkerchief and sometimes
remembered the sunscreen.
And you have my word: the next time
I come across a bunch of roses,
I'll stop and do whatever it is
you ask me to do next.

Exceptional Feet

He had a notable head of hair for his age,
not yet completely gray and wavy
in the week or so before he got a haircut,
but by far his best physical feature was his feet—
well-proportioned with a beautiful arch,
and ten straight toes of the perfect length
capped by pink, well-trimmed nails.
Very good cuticles. Like most men,
his feet were almost always cocooned in shoes,
even during the summer in his case
as he didn't especially care for flip-flops
and sandals. His exceptional feet
were visible for the world to admire
on the rare occasions he vacationed
at the beach, but at the beach there were
so many other best physical features
on display that his exceptional feet
didn't attract many second looks.
Still, he considered himself fortunate
to have such a truly striking pair of feet.
He liked looking at them in the bath,
and they were better than having ugly feet,
or no feet at all.

What to Do About My Bacteria

Every month I read something surprising
about what the trillions of guest workers
in my intestinal tract have been doing
to promote my general welfare.
Ratcheting up my immune system,
squirting out serotonin and dopamine—
so much more than simply turning
what I eat into absorbable slush.
Lately I've been feeling guilty about
not offering them the pathway
to full citizenship I know in my heart
they deserve, but I can't seem to find
my own pathway past the issues
citizenship would raise. For one,
my insistence on a continued role
for amoxicillin. For another,
their fondness for announcing
their presence in an overly exuberant
and generally inopportune manner.
And though they collectively weigh
only a few pounds, there are trillions
more of them than my natural-born cells…
what if they all vote as a block?

Peering into a Midwinter Sky

Tonight it's my own mind I see:
a vast expanse of empty space
dotted with ice-white points of light,

some dim, some bright, some few
of which may one day show
actual signs of intelligent life.

Great nebulous clouds of gas and dust,
hungry black holes swallowing up
everything, even the light.

The milky promise of something bigger.
All of it spinning inexorably toward
who knows what end.

The Quantum Fly

The fly banging against the window in my study
this morning makes me think of quantum tunneling,
the infinitesimally small but still real possibility
that all the atoms in an object (e.g. a housefly)
could simultaneously align in such a way that it will pass
unimpeded through a barrier (e.g. a pane of glass).

If ever a fly deserved such an outcome, it's the one
I'm watching. I've lost count of the times
it's crashed into the glass, buzzed down to the sill,
then swooped out for another run. Occasionally
it's made a soft landing on the glass and taken a quiet,
seemingly random stroll; only rarely has it remained
motionless on the pane, the strategy that would
maximize the odds of it tunneling to the other side.

The fly, of course, can't comprehend any of this.
Yet for all my greater powers of reason,
if the quantum stars miraculously aligned
in my room this morning, it's only the fly,
utterly ignorant of physics and probability,
that would simply accept the outcome
and get on with the rest of its day.

The Ultimate Nature of Reality

It unfolded before him maybe half the times he dropped acid. Even when he stood in its presence for only a few seconds, the experience was as utterly mind-blowing as you would expect standing in the presence of the Ultimate Nature of Reality to be. Trying to describe it to his friends afterward was as fruitless as reconstructing a burned-out building from the smoke lingering over the embers. One of his friends suggested he keep a pen and pad of paper next to him whenever he tripped. It was an excellent suggestion, except man, is it ever hard to remember to pick up a pen and pad of paper when you're about to stand in the presence of the Ultimate Nature of Reality. Eventually, though, he did remember; he picked up the pen and with great concentration wrote down what he perceived of the Ultimate Nature of Reality. The next morning, he was shocked to discover that the entire thing—the whole enchilada, the sum and essence of all that ever was and will be—could be expressed in two simple words, words he still has taped above his desk: *Cherry Tomato.*

The Pen

It was an inexpensive blue Bic
with a gel grip, but man, did I ever
love that pen; the smooth line flowing
like a felt tip, the perfect fit in my hand.
Over the years it authorized
a small fortune in credits and debits,
conveyed my warmest congratulations
and sincerest sympathies,
and dutifully recorded hundreds
of potentially remarkable insights
on napkins and envelopes.
When it finally ran out of ink
I performed a cartridge transplant
from a perfectly good donor pen
hiding in my desk. The old Bic
was never quite the same after that,
but I kept on using it anyway.
The evening I left it in a restaurant
with a credit card receipt,
I gave serious consideration
to driving back and telling the waitress
that pen was all I had managed
to salvage from the tragic fire
that had taken the life of my mother,
and perhaps also her dog.
It wasn't shame that stopped me,

but the sadness I'd perceived in the way
the waitress had moved that night;
a sadness that suggested she could use
a really good pen.

"I Can't Win for Losing"

It's what my father would say when
whatever he was trying to fix ended up
rattling or leaking more after he'd put down
his wrench than before he'd picked it up.
Depending on how many parts were involved,
that might come after an hour of contortions
or a whole afternoon, but hearing
those words at some point in the project
was one of my childhood's safer bets.

In his defense, there wasn't much need
for mechanical skills on an eastern Kentucky
hill farm during the Great Depression;
no electric wires or indoor plumbing to figure out,
and no machinery to do the work of backs
and arms. For the most part, too,
my father didn't say the words in anger,
but quietly, in the monotone of resignation.

I can't win for losing. In middle age
he started taping the words to his back
whenever he came across something in his life
he couldn't fix—wife, job, teenaged sons,
a country going to hell in a handbasket.

The phrase never made much sense to me.
Didn't *losing* just restate *I can't win*?
Where was the flash of pithy wisdom
the quaint use of *for* set up for delivery?
There wasn't any, of course, which I now
understand was the point.

Road Crew

I was the only one headed back
to college in ten weeks, and the only one
hired because his mother worked
in the company office. My sole job
was to shovel away the wet concrete
that spilled over the metal forms
framing the new third lane of I-83
north of Baltimore. It was hard,
shitty work, but I kept my head down
and came to enjoy sweating in the sun,
shirt off, the feel of new muscles
in my arms and back. In due course
the rest of the crew, six black men
who drove up from the city in a single Buick,
gave me the occasional nod.

Two of those men ran over to drag me
away from the cement spreader
the afternoon it crushed my right foot.
The old-timer called Slim pulled out a knife
and cut through the laces of my boot.
Miraculously, the x-rays taken in the ER
showed no bones had been broken.
Ashamed of my carelessness and not wanting
to lose the three days of pay before
worker's comp would kick in, I took

a single day of light duty at another site
then limped back to my crew.
I was sure such a display of grit
would make me a hero in their eyes,
but it was only one more way
I proved how little I knew.

I See Dead People

The first two were in the front seat of a Ford
that had issues with the downhill curve
leading into a West Virginia coal town.
I was ten, sitting with two of my brothers
in the back seat of a blue Chevy station wagon.
A quarter-mile from the Ford, traffic slowed
to a crawl, giving my father plenty of time
to work out what had happened. Closer in,
knots of locals leaned against old pick-ups,
sipping ten-ounce RC colas and pretending
not to enjoy the commotion.

In the Ford, a young woman in a flowered dress
slumped against the passenger's side window.
The driver, a dark-haired man of about the same age,
sprawled against the back of his seat, eyes closed,
face up, mouth open. There wasn't a mark
or speck of blood on either one of them;
no shattered glass and a little red pom-pom
still dangling from the rearview mirror.

But I knew—from the odd angle of their limbs,
and the way the four deputies stood around
smoking cigarettes while waving the cars past.
And there was an unfamiliar edge
in my mother's voice as she commanded us

not to look, then said *they're only sleeping*,
a statement I immediately recognized as a lie,
the first of many I'd be told in the interest
of sparing someone.

My Mother Wants a Gun

I'm eleven, summoned to the sofa with my brothers
to hear our mother swear she's going to get
a gun and blow her goddamn brains out
unless we stop doing this or start doing that
as of right this minute. My youngest brother
quakes under the barrage; the other three of us
struggle to keep our eyes on the carpet
and our various body parts from wiggling.
*Try using something bigger than a BB gun
this time*, I imagine myself telling her,
or P*lease, please, blow* my *brains out
so I don't have to sit through this again.*
Like any good smart-ass in the making,
I have dozens of such ripostes in my repertoire.

My youngest brother farts. Our mother
spins away in mid-invective, waves
her unlit cigarette at the ceiling uselessly,
then sputters into silence. For five long seconds,
everyone in the room rests in the uncertainty
of whether we're about to receive the mercy
or the back hand of God. Either way,
I'd say it was worth it.

The Starving Children
in Korea

By the time I was six there were no longer
enough starving children in Germany and Japan
to shame the children of east Baltimore
into eating the liver and onions on their plates.
Fortunately for the mothers of east Baltimore,
a new group of starving children had recently
been made available for service in Korea.

One particularly bleak evening I raised my head
to suggest that my mother scrape my lima beans
into a Tupperware and mail them to Korea.
From my limited understanding of geography
and the way the U.S. postal system worked,
that seemed like what would later be known
as a "win-win" situation; and it was clearly
better than my Plan B, which was to invite
some starving Korean kids over to our house.
I was apparently mistaken on several counts.

The Starving Children
in Vietnam

I can't remember
a single time
I or anyone I knew
invoked them
at our tables;
such was the price
they paid for
their parents' victory
and our progress.

Boys with Rocks

Every day after school we picked
the smoothest-edged stones
from the bulldozed moonscape
of a housing development gone bust,
expertly weighing each one
in the dusty scale of our palms
before turning it with thumb
and forefinger to find the perfect grip
for speed and spin.

Pick a target: it wouldn't take
any of us ten tries to hit
a telephone pole at seventy feet,
or shatter a beer bottle at fifty.
One afternoon when those targets
weren't enough to entertain us,
we set our sights on a small brown bird
perched far enough away to take
no account of our presence. *Shoot—*
what were the chances anyway?

Good enough that fifty years later
I sometimes still see the flutter
of that bird's wings when I pick up a rock
and cock back my arm.

Homeward Bound

On those sweltering mornings
when we left my grandfather's farm
for the long drive north, his final act
was to haul an old cardboard box
of mason jars and unwashed vegetables
to the gravel where we waited
to shuffle through awkward goodbyes.
The ritual of our departure required
my father to refuse the offering three times
before kissing his mother on the cheek
and wedging the box into the back
of our Chevy wagon.

Half a dirt mile later the box would be
one more entry in the bill of complaints
my mother was waiting to present,
situated somewhere after the Sears catalog
used for toilet paper in the outhouse,
the chicken shit littering the front yard,
and the nightly gospel radio music
played to brainwash us. *Christ,*
she'd say to my father while puffing
on her first cigarette in a week,
*one of these years you might mention
that we do have grocery stores in Maryland,
and enough money to shop in them.*

The potatoes, onions, and canned peaches
were close enough to our A&P diet
to find their way onto our table.
The jars of pickles, beets, and cabbage
were, however, left for my father to savor
in whatever way he chose—which was mostly
late at night in an unlit dining room,
one slow bite at a time, washed down
with Kentucky rye.

The Prisoner

He was captured crossing a pasture
on his 19th birthday, and spent
the next two days tied up in a farmhouse
while his guards smoked cigarettes
and bickered about whether to put a bullet
in his head or wait for the truck
that would carry him east. Before they
could settle the matter, he bolted
into the blackness of a Normandy night
when he was let into the garden
for his bedtime piss. From what
his family pieced together over the years,
he killed two German soldiers
with a bayonet in the seven days
it took to work his way back to friendly lines,
sick as the proverbial dog from a diet
of dandelions and pond water.

Sixty-five years later, his death
was the front-page story in the local paper.
The first nine paragraphs recounted
the details of his capture and heroic escape.
The tenth noted his successful career
in insurance and love of gardening,
the eleventh named his many family members,
and the final one listed the place
and times that visitors might call.

This was not a man I could say
I knew well—but something in the way
he stared out of the pictures by his coffin
left me thinking he'd have written
those paragraphs differently.

The Call of Duty

Though our mother
could hold her own
with a hairbrush or belt,
some of our childhood
crimes were so grievous
we had to wait for our father
to carry out the sentence.
He was an Army sergeant
in those years; and I
suppose you could say
it was to his credit
that no matter what
mood he came home in
or how inconspicuous
we managed to make
ourselves on seeing
that blue Chevy turn
into the driveway,
he always managed
to do his duty.

Hand Tools

I spent most of yesterday using the timber saw
I bought at an antique store to cut up half
of the oak tree last February's blizzard brought down.
This morning I'll haul the pieces to a place
near the house where I can use my equally ancient
splitting maul to turn them into firewood.

On such days I often imagine my grandfather
doing the same work in the Kentucky hills
where he raised his family in a four-room shack
without running water or electric power.
Wood was everywhere he looked, and free;
with five young mouths to feed, his choice was either
to put his back into splitting it or spend cash
for the coal he heaved into underground rail carts
five days a week, six when he was lucky.

I used to tell people my devotion to hand tools
was a kind of tribute to my grandfather's hard life,
but over time I came to see it as closer to mockery—
everyone in those Appalachian hills with a lick of sense,
including my grandfather, bought a chainsaw
and a gas-engine splitter as soon as they could
spare the money. Now when anyone asks,
I just say I've found that swinging a maul
is a good way to clear my mind.

Money

I miss having to have it
to get through the day—
the coins I tossed into toll baskets
and fed into vending machines,
the little stack of bills I could pull
from my wallet and count
to see precisely where I stood
that week. I miss sauntering
into a building and exchanging
pleasantries with the human
who could give me some.
I miss the possibility of nickels
and dimes under the seats
of my car, and forgotten wads
of ones and fives in the back
of my underwear drawer.
I miss having to look at it before
I handed it over for whatever
it was I was absolutely sure
I needed. I miss not having
every move I make authorized
by a goddamn machine.

See a Penny

I spot another one and amble over to pick it up,
a behavior that increasingly embarrasses
my wife. When I was a kid, I tell her yet again,
you could actually *buy* something with one of these—
a medium-sized jawbreaker, or a piece
of Bazooka bubble gum with a comic
in the wrapper. With five or ten of them,
I say ardently while jingling the coins
in my pocket for emphasis, you could eat
like a king—a full-sized Hershey bar
or a Mallow cup, or five of those little wax tubes
filled with something resembling Kool-Aid—
the possibilities were endless.

My wife again suggests that part of me
has spent the last fifty years living in a cave,
but I tell her that's not true; I realize the days
of buying things with pennies are long gone.
It's just that I can't for the life of me
understand how anyone could afford to pass up
the entire day of good luck picking up a penny
is known to bring. Even more so when
it's heads up.

State Road

Every morning at dawn I strolled down
the quarter-mile of our driveway
to fetch the paper and see what
the previous evening's tide of traffic
had washed onto the grass.
Not a day passed that I didn't find
half a dozen plastic bags and fast-food wrappers,
a couple of Bud Lite cans or Pepsi bottles.
Enough cigarette butts in the course
of a week to fill up a coffee cup,
enough losing lottery tickets to feed
a family of four. Every now and then
a music CD (heavy metal or country),
a soggy magazine (twice a *Playboy*),
or an unopened piece of a neighbor's mail.
Occasionally something useful:
several 2x4s, a dry bale of straw,
and the orange Philips-head screwdriver
I still have in a kitchen drawer.
One morning the puzzle of a pair of panties,
silky red with white hearts (size M).
For all the hundreds of bottles,
not a single one with a message inside.

Three

1:30 AM Saturday Morning

I pop open another beer and ask
the Internet for news of Myself.
As I suspected, I'm mostly the same.
I still own a furniture store
outside Cincinnati and a thriving
personal injury law practice in Florida.
Last month a newspaper in Maine
published a letter to the editor
on an issue I apparently have
very strong feelings about.
There's no evidence anywhere
that I've been appointed to an important
government task force, which,
truthfully, is a relief at this point.
On a sad note, I see that I just passed away
in Baltimore after a lengthy illness;
I should probably send flowers.

On a Day When Nothing Pleases Me, I Think of Mary Oliver*

On a day when nothing pleases me,
I drag myself outside for the opportunity
to not be pleased with the stifling heat
and humidity of a mid-August afternoon.
Once there, I decide to not be pleased
with taking a walk down the same trail
I walked down yesterday so I can listen
to the same-old same-old song
of the same creek I sat by yesterday.

As I make the last turn, however,
I'm stopped dead in my tracks by a scene
straight out of a Mary Oliver poem.
Not one, but *two* herons fishing in the water
thirty feet in front of me. A loose chevron
of wild geese honking by overhead.
At the water's edge, a grasshopper clinging
to the tip of a tall blade of grass.

I'll admit it's a lovely interlude
on a day when nothing seems to please me.
But it's not nearly enough to keep me
from wondering whether Mary has ever
secretly wanted to do what I do next—

---

* A very popular New England nature poet.

which is to point my right index finger
at the lead goose, squint down my arm,
and cock back my thumb.

Viva la Revolución

A screen mounted to the end of one
of the cleaning products aisles in Walmart
is playing a video extolling a revolutionary
new way of getting those hard-to-remove stains
out of clothes. I saunter over to watch,
pulled in by the image of the attractive young woman
explaining how the host of animated bubbles
do their amazing work. Her bouncy tone
and toothy smile convey actual enthusiasm
for revolutionizing the way the world removes
especially difficult clothing stains.
Over the years I've listened to hundreds
of similar pitches with no complaint,
but lately their use of the word *revolutionary*
has been bothering me. How, I ask myself,
did that word slide from describing
causes people took to the streets for
to laundry soaps, skin creams, and car tires?
It sure as hell isn't because the world
ran out of *revolucións* in need of some *viva*.
Looking out over the expanse of aisles,
I realize how much I miss the old use
of *revolutionary*. I want it restored—
immediately and without preconditions,
and am even willing to live with soaps
that are merely remarkable
to get it back.

Shovels

The first one I bought was the only one I've owned that had a piece of steel welded across the back to keep dirt from clogging up the shank. Nothing could slice through the ground like the blade of that shovel; it was practically an extension of my arms as I learned how to garden in our first years living in the country. One rainy Saturday in March, I used it to plant more than a hundred tree seedings at the far end of the field our kitchen window looked out on. Shortly after moving to our second house, I stupidly broke the hickory handle trying to pry a cherry stump out of the ground. The piece left in the shank was held tightly in place by a metal dowel hammered flat on both ends. By that point in my life I had more money than time, so I drove to the local hardware store and bought whatever shovel I found hanging on their back wall. Eventually I threw out the pieces of the broken shovel, a decision I have since had plenty of time to regret.

Calculators

I'm staring blankly at two columns of numbers,
trying once again to hand crank the machinery
of basic mathematics I mothballed back
when I bought the brick-sized calculator
that was going to liberate my mind
for higher-order problem-solving tasks.
In retrospect, that wasn't such a great trade-off;
I can think of plenty of mornings when
doing long division in my head
would have proved useful, but none when
I've needed to figure out the precise time
and place two trains moving toward each other
at different speeds would meet.
And I have yet to churn with resentment
at being dependent on my head, which I also
have never left the house without.

Refrigerators

There's a woman down the street who at 82
can tell you the exact amount her late husband
paid for the white refrigerator two men
from Sears delivered to their house 39 years ago.
Like her, it's still chugging away in the same kitchen,
starting and stopping with a little more effort
than when it first arrived, but somehow
managing to do what it was designed to do.
Five years ago I tried to convince her
that a new model would pay for itself in no time
by using less electricity, plus she'd get
a $150 rebate check direct from the entity
she insists on calling "the gas company."
I might as well have been teaching her calculus.
This morning I'm bringing her up to speed
on digital temperature displays and the magic
of getting water and ice (cubed *or* crushed)
right from the door, a wonderful convenience
in this day and age. She nods and tries in her way
to look interested, but it's plain she's
not paying a bit of attention. All I can do
is nod back as she pats my arm and explains
that when it comes to things you plug in,
she's found that you can't need
what you don't know.

A Teachable Moment

My son tells me the last ordeal
of the wilderness training he'd just completed
was to spend three full days
in the woods with only this to eat—
a little cheese and pepperoni,
some crackers, a small bag of trail mix,
and a handful or two of peanut M&Ms.
I start mentally rationing that out
across the three days while he practices
his knots with a length of nylon rope.
Before I can launch into my lecture
on how I would have handled things,
he mentions that he ate the whole stash
right after he woke up on the first morning.
I frown and deliver my lecture anyway;
then concede he'd be right to say
I would have spent the whole three days
only slightly less hungry than he
spent two.

The Last Time We Carried Our Children

They fell asleep in the back seat of our Toyota wagon
on the long drive home from a November visit
to your parents. They'd romped around outside
with their cousins all day, and in the car still
smelled of leaf. The sound of our voices rehashing
the who said what of the day's conversations
made their heads droop before we were over the dam.
In front of us, the sky changed slowly from
cotton-candy pink to the speckled black of night.
I parked in the driveway and ran ahead
to unlock the front door while you fumbled
with their seat buckles. I carried our daughter
into the house against my shoulder, her legs
dangling at my thighs; you could still just manage
our son cradled to your chest.

It might well have happened like that, but who
really knows? There's only so much you can see
looking in a rearview mirror.

A Potentially Quite Remarkable Encounter

I'm sitting on a bench in the main square
of my college town when I'm startled to see
my student self walking directly toward me.
Even after so many years, there's no mistaking him—
the tailored, forest-green army dress jacket
he bought for 35 cents at a second-hand shop,
a blue McGovern pin still loitering on the left lapel,
that long, brisk stride masquerading as purpose,
the way his head hangs down as if he's lost
in thought about important matters.
He'd be shocked by how little of what
I want to tell him about the road ahead
has to do with anything his 20-year-old brain
might think to ask.

When he's a few steps away I startle him
with a friendly greeting and an invitation
to *please, come join me.* He slows just enough
to give a quizzical nod back and then hurries on
to his favorite spot by the river, shoulders hunched,
hands tucked in the pockets of his jeans
to ward off the chill.

Picture This

The young couple sitting next to me
is debating where they had dinner
on the first night of a trip they'd taken
right after they met a few years ago.
As they talk, their index fingers scroll past
screen after screen of tiny pictures
until first one and then the other
arrives at the precise time and place
in question. Satisfied by what they see,
they swipe a few more times and point
and laugh, and move quickly on
to some other topic.

I'm of an age that I'd be hard-pressed
to find even a single printed picture
memorializing events in my life
far bigger than my companion's dinner.
Even so, there's something to be said
for having a past riddled with gaps
that only imagination or a long evening
of wine and conversation can fill;
a past you cannot browse, but must
think about and tell.

Gone with the Wind

Back then neither of us would have guessed
the details of that night could ever fade—
the drive in my yellow Toyota to see
Gone with the Wind, a movie we'd discussed
but which you'd somehow never seen;
the long talk in your dorm room afterward;
the shock of the kiss that has yet to end.

Passing a few miles from our college town
forty years later, neither of us can remember
whether we saw the movie at the theater in Church Hill
or the one further down the road in Centreville.
There's time in our schedule for a side trip,
where we're pleased to find both buildings
still standing and in use as community arts centers.
We consider their merits as we start for home,
and agree it must have been the one in Centreville.

And what did knowing this possibly matter?
Only someone who hadn't seen the movie
would need to ask.

Days We'll Never Forget

I'm barely eight in my first one,
fidgeting at a desk and wondering
why the principal is so upset
as she quivers out the news
that the President has been shot.
I mean it's not like he's an Indian
or a cowboy with a black mustache
that a bullet could put down for the count;
I'm fully expecting to see him
on tonight's episode of the NBC news
with a sling cradling his left arm,
or maybe a white bandage around his head
with a dark spot on one temple.
Before she leaves, the principal leads us
in a moment of silent prayer
during which I beseech Jesus to let us
out early. Miraculously, He does—
one more small thing about that day
I didn't know I would remember
for the rest of my life.

The Hour of God

I sit at my bedroom window
on a winter night too wide to cross
in a single sleep, looking out
on a world that even at this hour
is filled with porch lights
and the pale blue flicker of screens,
the slow sweep of headlights
coming and of taillights going.
Miles above me, a hundred people
blink slowly toward the horizon.
Centuries ago, the devout called this
the Hour of God, the time when
the dark stillness of the earth
invited Him close enough for the wordless
conversations of the heart.
How strange, I think, that our lights
are what now keep Him from us.

Out of Synch

Well shit. I'm only exhibiting four of the *7 Habits for a Happier Life* and I don't regularly eat more than half of the *12 Superfoods Guaranteed to Boost Your Energy*. I wasn't smart enough to pick one of *The 50 Best Places for Retirement*, and the clock is ticking on my vague plan to visit the *30 Places You Must See Before You Die*. I worry that I should be investing at least a little time in mastering *The 5 Secrets to Attracting Women* in case the one I have detects any of *The 7 Red Flags Your Marriage Is in Trouble*, one of which is fortunately not that *You've Been Clipping Your Fingernails All Wrong*, because apparently I have been, I have. As a matter of principle I refuse to memorize the *6 Signs Your Memory Problems Are Not Normal*. I can, however, recite every one of the *9 Reasons You Should Take a Nap Right Now*. And when I wake up, I'm going to pour a second cup of coffee before anyone can declare *The 5 Health Benefits of Caffeine* null and void.

After a Hard Day's Work at the Creek

I soothe aching,
thorn-scraped limbs
in steaming water,
lie naked

between clean white sheets,
listen to the sounds
of an April dusk
descending.

The delicate fragrance
of those sheets—
their crisp coolness
against my skin—

I could lie there
with my eyes closed
forever—

though perhaps
not just
yet.

Trains

As a boy I'd lie in the bedroom
of a sweltering Baltimore rowhouse
listening to the slow clack
of the freight trains a mile or so away,
imagining myself riding them
to some great open landscape—
Nebraska maybe, where I'd jump off
and point my feet toward the water tower
on the horizon, everything I owned
in the knapsack on my back, heart racing
with the excitement of not being
dependent on nobody else for nothin'.
Most of a lifetime later I'd still say
the far-off wail of a train whistle
is the most beautiful sound I can hear
in the late hours of a quiet night,
though more now for the sweetness
of the memories it stirs
than for the mystery of where
it could take me.

Returning to the Creek Trail

Three years of neglect was all it took
to erase the months of hard labor
I'd put into scratching that trail
out of the thick tangles
of brush and vines smothering
the quarter-mile of steep ground
winding back up to the house,

all those quiet evening hours
spent clearing downed branches
and clipping each spring's
new growth with the pruners
I carried in a back pocket.

Three years gone and barely
a trace of what I'd done remaining;
I turned back to my car not sure
whether I should be comforted by that
or dismayed.

Oration

In the distance, the staccato drumroll
of a neighbor's mower. I approach the ladder
and begin the long ascent to asphalt shingles,
an autumn wind stirring the expanse of trees
pressed up against the lawn. On the roof,
I plant my feet, pivot slowly to face the trees,
and take a moment to collect myself.
The mower stops. The wind dies down.
Two squirrels standing on their hind legs
stare at me from the edge of the grass.
A squadron of crows flutters into silence
on the top branch of a dying oak.
I have an uneasy feeling some words
are expected. But what? An exhortation?
A confession? A prayer?

Pain

Mine has been of the ordinary kind.
I have not lived years closeted in darkness,
shoulders bent with the weight of a lie.
I have not had to choose food over heat,
medicine over decent shoes. My brain
and all my body parts still work more or less
as intended. Sure, my parents
could have loved me better, and I them;
but that was a long time ago.
My worst wounds were self-inflicted,
and healed nicely when I left them alone.
A few of the scars are quite fetching,
but I am long past the point
of having any need to show them.

The State of Things

Things aren't going well in the world;
people blowing themselves up
for god and the ice caps melting.
Not enough good jobs
and everybody shouting.
But if you ask me
how I am this evening
I'll say fine, thank you.
We had a record snow
for December and the power
stayed on. I ate a bowl
of hearty bean soup for dinner.
I climbed into the attic
and brought down
the mouse traps I'd set.
It's a good night
for mercy.

Acknowledgements

Thanks to my dear wife Susan and friends Martha and Robert Orton for their thoughtful comments on the poems in this collection, and to Sarah Crossland for her usual excellent work in transforming the manuscript into an appealing book. Thanks, too, to neighbor Jeff Grotsky, whose real-life battle with buzzards inspired the poem that provided a perfect title for the book.

Photo credit: Carolyne Grotsky

www.ingramcontent.com/pod-product-compliance
Lightning Source LLC
Chambersburg PA
CBHW051841040426
42447CB00006B/647